D0258472

# Maths
# without
# worksheets

## Maths through painting, role play and more

Brenda Whittle and Heidi Jayne

For ages
3–5

**Authors**
Brenda Whittle and Heidi Jayne

**Development Editor**
Simret Brar

**Editor**
Margaret Eaton

**Assistant Editor**
Alex Albrighton

**Series Designer**
Anna Oliwa

**Designer**
Geraldine Reidy

**Cover Illustration**
Craig Cameron/Art Collection

**Illustrations**
Gaynor Berry

Text © 2008 Brenda Whittle and Heidi Jayne
© 2008 Scholastic Ltd

Designed using Adobe InDesign

Published by Scholastic Ltd
Villiers House
Clarendon Avenue
Leamington Spa
Warwickshire
CV32 5PR

www.scholastic.co.uk

Printed by Bell & Bain Ltd, Glasgow

1 2 3 4 5 6 7 8 9    8 9 0 1 2 3 4 5 6 7

**British Library Cataloguing-in-Publication Data**
A catalogue record for this book is available from the British Library.

ISBN 978-0439-94558-5

## Acknowledgement

The publishers gratefully acknowledge permission to reproduce the following copyright material:
**Janet Perry** for the use of 'I Am A Robot' by Janet Perry © 2008, Janet Perry (2007, previously unpublished).

Her Majesty's Stationery Office for the use of extracts from *Practice Guidance for the Early Years Foundation Stage* © Crown copyright, reproduced under the terms of the Click-Use Licence.

Every effort has been made to trace copyright holders for the works reproduced in this book, and the publishers apologise for any inadvertent omissions.

# Contents

## Counting and calculating

## Shape, space and measures

## Open the box!

# Introduction

## Maths without worksheets

*Maths without worksheets* is one of a series of books containing 'outside the box' ideas for practitioners working with children in the early years. Children's interests and joy for life form the basis for the activities in this series. The activities build on children's natural instinct to be doing, investigating, making, creating and solving problems. They are designed to excite and stimulate children as they learn through their senses, being active and thinking for themselves.

### But why maths without worksheets?

The emphasis in this book is on children's enjoyment of developing mathematical understanding through very varied indoor and outdoor activities that are fun, challenging and exciting. At times, children may want or be encouraged to record what they have done in ways meaningful to them. This could be through drawings, tallying or using numbers, but they are not asked to complete 'one size fits all'

worksheets that may limit or constrain their mathematical thinking.

### Wanting to use mathematical knowledge and skills

The activities are designed to capture children's imaginations so that they cannot wait to get started, to experiment, reason, solve problems, ask questions and make connections between numeracy and other areas of their learning. When children realise that using their mathematical knowledge and skills to reason and solve problems is enjoyable and empowering, they grow in confidence and competence.

### How to use this book

The book is organised into three sections:
● Chapter 1: 'Numbers, counting and calculating' includes lively activities that are designed to give opportunities for children to sort, count, recognise numerals and solve problems involving addition and subtraction. The children help a park keeper

count and plant flowers, order the 10 to 0 'countdown' cards at the space station ready for a rocket to take off, or solve number problems as the King or Queen of Hearts.

● Chapter 2: 'Shape, space and measures' introduces children to the wonderful world of shape, space and measures as they solve problems such as finding the longest and shortest necklaces in the messy princess's jewellery box, recognise numerals as they 'rock' around a giant-sized outdoor clock, or become firefighters filling buckets and containers with water.

● Chapter 3: 'Open the box!' presents children with a variety of intriguing boxes and bags that each pose mathematical problems for them to solve. They learn about size and shape when they make blankets for Big Bear and Little Bear, use positional language when they use the toolbox to repair broken-down vehicles, or sort and count the contents of the teacher's bag that have spilled onto the table.

## The activities
### Planning and learning objectives
Links to the Development Matters and Early Learning Goals for Problem solving, reasoning and numeracy (PSRN) in the DfES document *Practice Guidance for the Early Years Foundation Stage* are shown for each activity to aid planning. The activities are all cross-curricular and the main link to one of the other five Areas of Learning is also shown where appropriate.

### Support and extension
Each activity has suggestions for how it may be adapted or extended according to children's needs and stage of development.

### Assessment
Practitioners can assess children's progress against the objectives and Early Learning Goals shown for each activity. Most of the activities are designed for small groups, enabling practitioners to observe individual children's progress and aid assessment to inform future planning.

### Further activities
These provide more suggestions for developing lively activities linked to the main activity.

### Play links
Ideas for play-linked learning to the main activity are given to continue the theme into other Areas of Learning, such as opportunities for investigations or role play.

### Home links
In order to promote and foster a partnership with parents or carers for the benefit of the children, a suggestion is given in each activity to link the learning in the setting to that in the home.

### Health and safety
Follow the health and safety guidelines in place for your particular setting or local authority.

### Abbreviations
References to Areas of Learning in the DfES document *Practice Guidance for the Early Years Foundation Stage:*
● Personal social and emotional development (PSED)
● Communication, language and literacy (CLL)
● Problem solving, reasoning and numeracy (PSRN)
● Knowledge and understanding of the world (KUW)
● Physical development (PD)
● Creative development (CD)

# Counting and calculating

## Helping Sam

**In this activity, children help out a busy park keeper who has left them a list of jobs to do that involve counting, planting and watering.**

### What you need

Laminated copies of the lists featured on photocopiable page 7; children's gardening tools (wheelbarrow, trowels, forks, watering can); plastic plant pots; compost; assorted artificial flowers.

### Learning objectives

**Numbers as Labels and for Counting**
● Count up to six objects from a larger group. **(PSRN)**
● Recognise numerals 1 to 5. **(PSRN)**
● Know that numbers identify how many objects are in a set. **(PSRN)**

**Early Learning Goals**
● Count reliably up to ten everyday objects. **(PSRN)**
● Recognise numerals 1 to 9. **(PSRN)**

**Early mathematicians** count up to five objects with adult support.
**More confident mathematicians** count up to ten objects and recognise the numerals 1 to 9.

### What to do

● Tell the children that Sam, a busy park keeper, has asked if they will help him out and he has left a list of jobs for them to do. Show them one of Sam's lists (see photocopiable page 7) and ask them to help you work out what they will need. Identify each item from the illustration and read the numeral to see how many of each item they will need. Count the pieces of equipment, load them into the wheelbarrow and set off to the garden area where a bag of compost is ready to use. Count the items as you unload them and show the children how to fill the pots with compost. Plant and water the flowers.
● Use the flowers as the basis for further counting activities by asking questions: *How many red flowers are there? Are there more red flowers than yellow flowers?* Make sure that the children wash their hands thoroughly at the end of the activity.

### Support and extension

● Tell younger children how many of each item you need, rather than using the lists. Support the children by touching each object as you count together.
● Encourage older children to work independently as they count the correct number of items they need and decide how many flowers to plant in each pot.

### Further activity

Improve the outdoor area by planting and caring for a pot of real flowers. Encourage the children to count the plants, monitor their growth and enjoy their colours and scent.

### Play link

Provide plastic straws, sticky tape, card, paints and scissors for children to make and cut out flowers, taping them to the straws as stems.

### Home link

Suggest that parents or carers interest their children in counting activities by counting trees on the way to the setting or in a park.

### Cross-curricular links

**Exploration and Investigation**
● Show an awareness of change. **(KUW)**
**Early Learning Goal**
● Look closely at similarities differences, patterns and change. **(KUW)**

# Helping Sam

SCHOLASTIC
www.scholastic.co.uk

# Naughty numbers

**In this activity, children paint giant-sized numbers and discover the next day that the numbers have hidden themselves around the setting. They search for the numbers and try to identify them from the parts they see peeping out from their hiding places.**

**Early mathematicians** recognise and write the numerals 1 to 5 with adult support.
**More confident mathematicians** recognise and write the numerals 1 to 9 independently.

## What you need
Large sheets of paper or card; ready-mixed paints; thick brushes; scissors; 1 to 9 number cards.

## What to do
● Sing counting songs and rhymes together, such as '1, 2, 3, 4, 5, Once I caught a fish alive!' or 'One, two, buckle my shoe', pointing to the appropriate numbers on the number cards during the songs. Encourage the children to look carefully at the shapes of the numbers, noticing the straight and curved lines. Ask them to choose and identify one of the numbers and draw it with their 'magic finger' in different places around the room, such as in the air, on the floor or on someone else's back.

● Ask the children to choose one or more numbers, select paint colours and paint the numbers, giant-sized. Identify and talk about the numbers. Cut out each number and tell the children that you are leaving the pile of numbers ready for the next day.
● Before the children arrive for the next session, hide the numbers around the setting, with just a small part of each one visible – for example, hiding them behind posters, inside books, under a table and so on.
● When the children arrive, explain that the numbers are missing. Where can they have gone? Are they hiding? Search the setting together, looking for the

numbers. As the children find a number, ask them to try to identify it by looking at the shape of the small part that is visible. Slowly reveal the rest of the number, until they work out which it is. When all of the numbers have been found, make them into a number line to display in the corridor or cloakroom area.

### Support and extension
● Support younger children in recognising numerals from 1 to 5 that are significant to them.
● Encourage older children to paint numbers 1 to 9 and above, picking out numbers with particular significance, such as their house numbers.

### Further activities
● Provide a Naughty Numbers box to use outside, containing plastic numbers, coloured chalks, pots of water and thick brushes. Encourage some children to hide the numbers and others to search for them. When they find them, the searchers should

draw or paint the numbers onto the hard play surface using chalks or water.
● Drop plastic numbers into a bucket of bubbly water. Ask a child to bring a number slowly to the surface, revealing just a small part of it through the bubbles. Ask the other children to try to identify the number.

### Play link
Provide card, glue, glue brushes and collage materials such as sand, glitter, sequins, buttons and so on. Ask the children to draw numbers using the glue and brushes and then cover them with collage materials. When dry, cut out the number shapes and hang them from a coat hanger to make a mobile. **(CD)**

### Home link
Encourage the children to be number searchers at home, looking for numbers on the television or food packets.

> ### Cross-curricular links
> **Exploring Media and Materials**
> ● Choose particular colours to use for a purpose. **(CD)**
> **Early Learning Goal**
> ● Explore colour, texture, shape, form and space in two or three dimensions. **(CD)**

# Dance with dinosaurs

**After sharing a lively story about dinosaurs, the children sort and count their own dinosaurs as they dance them away to a party.**

## What you need

*Bumpus Jumpus Dinosaurumpus!* by Tony Mitton and Guy Parker-Rees (Orchard Picturebooks); assorted toy dinosaurs (or see photocopiable page 11); coloured paper cut-outs representing caves, pools and fields.

## What to do

● Share the book *Bumpus Jumpus Dinosaurumpus!* with the children, spending time talking about each type of dinosaur, the sounds they make and the way they move. Encourage the children to enjoy the rhythm of the text and join in with the refrain:

Shake, shake, shudder...
near the sludgy old
swamp.
The dinosaurs are coming.
Get ready to romp.

● Spread out the paper caves, pools and grass and put the collection of dinosaurs in the middle. (If you are using the illustrations from photocopiable page 11, copy the sheet onto different-coloured paper, then cut out and laminate the dinosaur shapes.) Sort through the dinosaurs together, talking about their colours, sizes and shapes. Refer to the book and comment how the same types of dinosaurs came along to the dinosaurumpus together. Ask the children to help you sort their dinosaurs into groups by different criteria such as 'all the red ones' or 'all the ones with horns'. Arrange the groups of dinosaurs in the caves, pools and grass. Count how many dinosaurs are in each group. Ask: *Which group has the most? Which has the least?*

● When the dinosaurs are sorted and in different areas, play some lively dance music and ask the children to join in with the refrain as they 'stomp' them along to the dinosaurumpus.

## Support and extension

● Support younger children by talking about the colours, sizes and other features of the dinosaurs as they begin to sort them.
● Encourage older children to choose their own criteria for sorting the dinosaurs and count how many are in each group.

## Further activity

Provide paper, ready-mixed paints and scissors for children to paint and cut out their own dinosaurs to cause a rumpus. Use these to make a sorting and counting display.

## Play link

Create your own dinosaurumpus as the children move like the dinosaurs in the story. The dinosaurs dance and sing until they are so tired they slow down and eventually fall asleep. **(CD)**

## Home link

Encourage the children to sort things at home, such as fruit in a bowl, socks in a drawer or money in a purse.

**Early mathematicians** begin to sort dinosaurs by given criteria, with adult support.
**More confident mathematicians** choose their own criteria for sorting dinosaurs and count the number in each group.

**Learning objective**
**Numbers as Labels and for Counting**
● Match then compare the number of objects in two sets. **(PSRN)**
● Count an irregular arrangement of up to ten objects. **(PSRN)**
**Early Learning Goal**
● Use developing mathematical ideas and methods to solve practical problems. **(PSRN)**

**Cross-curricular links**
**Language for Communication**
● Listen to stories with increasing attention and recall. **(CLL)**
**Early Learning Goal**
● Listen with enjoyment and respond to stories. **(CLL)**

# Dinosaurs

SCHOLASTIC
www.scholastic.co.uk

# A bunch of flowers

**This activity provides opportunities for the children to use their senses as they paint and count scented flowers for a market stall and label the vases with numerals made from scented play dough.**

**Early mathematicians** begin to count up to five flowers and recognise some numerals.
**More confident mathematicians** count up to ten flowers, create their own numerals and make a number line.

## What you need

Scented flowers (in a garden or bunch); ready-mixed paints; brushes; paper; scissors; lengths of garden cane; sticky tape; play dough; scents such as lavender and rose; set of plastic or laminated 1 to 9 numerals; child-safe vases.

## What to do

● Check that children do not have allergies before starting this activity. Set up one table for scented painting and one for scented play dough. Either take the children outside to see and smell flowers as they are growing or show them a bunch of scented flowers. Talk about the scents, colours and textures of the flowers.
● Explain to the children that they will be making scented paints to paint their own

flowers. Encourage them to smell the scents and help you add a little scent to the paints. Tell them that you want them to paint lots of flowers that they can then cut out and put into vases to make a flower stall. Help them tape their flower heads to pieces of garden cane and stand them in vases.
● Work a little scent into the play dough and encourage the children to enjoy smelling and moulding it. Give them the opportunity to experiment in moulding the play dough into the shapes of the numerals 1 to 9, referring to the laminated number cards.
● Ask the children to count the flowers in the vases. Tell them that you want them to label each vase with the correct number so

that the stall-holder knows how many flowers there are. They can paint or draw numbers for labels or make play dough number outlines. Leave the laminated numbers on the table to help the children remember the shapes of the numbers. As the children complete a number they should put it next to the correct vase, counting the flowers again. Give them time to enjoy smelling the painted flowers and numbers.

### Support and extension
● Help younger children count up to five flowers and make marks on paper or paint pictures to represent numbers.
● Challenge older children to make play dough numbers and use these to create their own number line.

### Further activities
● Provide a set of 1 to 9 numerals and a variety of materials for the children to manipulate to make their own numerals. These might include assorted pipe cleaners, plastic modelling material or clay. Remind the children to take care when using the sharp points of pipe cleaners.
● Make sure the children wash their hands

and you have a hygienic food preparation area. Make up a bread mix and give each child a piece of dough. Encourage them to choose a number that is significant to them (for example, their age) and mould the dough into that number shape. When the bread is cooking ask the children if they can smell it. When it is cool, enjoy the smell, texture and taste of the bread.

### Play link
Encourage the children to participate in role play, using the flowers they made for the market stall. Introduce a till, money, purses and wrapping paper so that they can take on the roles of stall-holder and customers. **(CD)**

### Home link
Suggest that parents or carers encourage their children to look for numbers they recognise when out shopping – for example, on a birthday card display or on the till display at the checkout.

**Cross-curricular links**
**Exploration and Investigation**
● Show curiosity and interest in the features of objects and living things. **(KUW)**
**Early Learning Goal**
● Investigate objects and materials by using all of their senses as appropriate. **(KUW)**

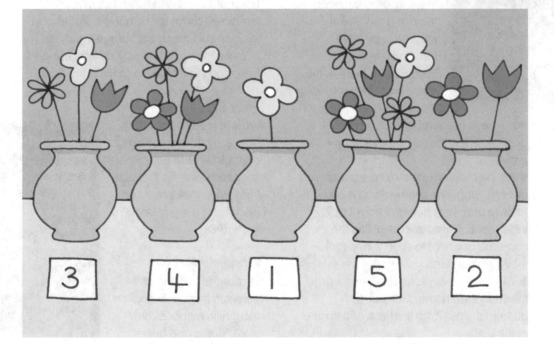

# Juicy fruits

**In this activity, children recognise numerals and enjoy using their senses as they make and eat numeral shapes made out of tangerine segments.**

## What you need
Tangerines; 1 to 9 numeral cards; laminated fruit bowl cards (see photocopiable page 15).

## What to do
● Before undertaking the following activities, make sure that all surfaces are safe for food preparation and that the children wash their hands and wear clean aprons. Check that they do not have food allergies or special dietary requirements.

● Ask the children to hold the tangerines, describing their colour, texture and smell. Show them how to peel the fruit and separate the segments. Count the number of segments together as you place them in a row. Ask the children to peel the remaining fruits, encouraging them to talk about what they are doing. Ask: *Does each tangerine have the same number of segments? Is it easier to count the segments in a row or a group?*

● Tell the children to watch carefully as you arrange tangerine segments on a board or table to make any numeral from 1 to 9. When the children have identified the numeral, ask them to choose and make their own numerals.

● When the activity is finished, encourage the children to name, then eat, the numerals, describing the taste and texture of the fruit.

**Learning objectives**
**Numbers as Labels and for Counting**
● Recognise numerals 1 to 5. **(PSRN)**
● Count up to three or four objects by saying one number name for each item. **(PSRN)**
**Early Learning Goals**
● Recognise numerals 1 to 9. **(PSRN)**
● Count reliably up to ten everyday objects. **(PSRN)**

## Support and extension
● Help younger children count the segments and stand 1 to 5 numeral cards near the table for them to refer to.
● Play the fruit bowl game with four children. Copy photocopiable page 15 onto orange paper. Cut out and laminate the shapes of the bowl and the separate tangerines. Give each player a 'fruit bowl' and place four sets of the 'tangerines' (24 cards) in the middle of the table. The children take it in turns to throw a dot or numbered dice, picking up the matching numbered tangerine and placing it on the appropriate space in their fruit bowl. The child who fills their fruit bowl first is the winner.

## Further activity
Fill small bowls with halved cherry tomatoes, carrot sticks, halved grapes and sticks of cucumber. Encourage the children to make 'number snacks' to share, using the fruits and vegetables to make numerals.

## Play link
Provide teddy bears, party hats, play dough, rolling pins, plates and number-shaped cutters for the children to make number biscuits for a teddy bears' party. **(PD)**

## Home link
Encourage parents and carers to help their children recognise numbers on signs, doors and buses.

**Cross-curricular links**
**Exploration and Investigation**
● Describe and talk about what they see. **(KUW)**
**Early Learning Goal**
● Find out about, and identify, some features of living things, objects and events they observe. **(KUW)**

# Fruit bowl game

SCHOLASTIC
www.scholastic.co.uk

# Penny patterns

**In this activity, children discover a trail of pennies and suggest who may have dropped them. Could it be Burglar Bill? They count the pennies and use them to trace over patterns.**

**Early mathematicians** experience handling coins, counting and tracing over the playground patterns. **More confident mathematicians** say the number that is one more than a given number and count more than ten coins.

## What you need

A copy of *Burglar Bill* by Janet and Allan Ahlberg (Picture Puffins); large sheets of paper; a large collection of 1p coins; bags for money.

## What to do

● In the week prior to this activity, share the story *Burglar Bill* with the children. Before the session, draw a variety of patterns to include straight, curved and dotted lines, spirals or shapes, onto large sheets of paper on the floor. Scatter a trail of pennies on the floor.

● When the children arrive, tell them that you have just found the coins and think someone must have dropped them. Encourage them to speculate by asking questions, such as: *Who could have dropped the coins? Did they have a hole in*

*their pocket? Could it have been Burglar Bill?* Ask the children to estimate how many pennies they think there are: *Could there be hundreds, thousands, millions?* Encourage the children to examine the coins and work out that they are 1p coins, by identifying the numeral on each one.

● Give each child a bag and ask them to help by counting the pennies into their bag, encouraging them to count above ten, if they can. When the coins are all collected, tell the children that you have an idea. Explain that you have drawn lots of patterns onto a big sheet of paper and you were going to ask the children to trace along them with buttons, but the pennies will be even better.

**Learning objectives**
**Numbers as Labels and for Counting**
● Count aloud in ones, twos, fives or tens. **(PSRN)**
● Count up to three or four objects by saying one number for each item. **(PSRN)**
● Begin to count beyond 10. **(PSRN)**
**Early Learning Goal**
● Say and use number names in order in familiar contexts. **(PSRN)**

● Invite the children to trace their fingers along the patterns, describing the lines as straight, curved, wavy, long or short. Gather the children together and ask them how many coins they think they will need to cover one of the patterns. Show them how to place the coins on the line, counting as you do so, or ask: *If we add one more, how many will we have?* Give the children time to enjoy covering the patterns, counting and talking about what they are doing.

## Support and extension
● Support younger children by counting with them as they place each coin on the line.
● Challenge older children to place coins side by side on the lines and begin to count in twos.

## Further activities
● Prepare games for a penny fair. These could include throwing a ball into a bucket, jumping inside a row of hoops, using a fishing net to catch plastic ducks in a water tray and so on. The children take turns in being stall-holders or paying one penny to have a go. At the end of the activity, count the pennies collected on each stall.
● Empty out a purse of assorted coins. Talk about the sizes, colours and shapes of the coins and look for the numerals on each one. Encourage the children to sort, identify or count them. If possible, go to a local shop and use the coins to buy something.

## Play link
Provide the children with chalks to create their own giant-sized patterns on the outdoor play area. Challenge them to cover the lines with bricks, bean bags or quoits, encouraging them to count as they do so. **(PSRN)**

## Home link
Suggest that parents or carers involve their children in handling money.

### Cross-curricular links
**Using Equipment and Materials**
● Show respect for other children's personal space when playing among them. **(PD)**
● Engage in activities requiring hand-eye coordination. **(PD)**
**Early Learning Goals**
● Show awareness of space, of themselves and of others. **(PD)**
● Handle tools, objects, construction and malleable materials safely and with increasing control. **(PD)**

# The Princess and the Pea

**Children are encouraged to find out if their princess doll is a real princess by hiding a pea under her mattress. They keep adding 'one more' mattress to see if she can still feel the bump made by the pea.**

## What you need
A copy of the fairy tale 'The Princess and the Pea'; a 'princess' doll; doll's bed; thin sponge washing-up pads (to use as mattresses); green play dough (for the pea).

## What to do
● Share the story of 'The Princess and the Pea' with the children, talking about the illustrations and the way the mattresses are piled on top of each other to cover the bump made by the pea. Introduce the 'princess' doll to the group and remind the children that if she is a real princess she will be able to feel the pea under all of the mattresses.
● Begin to retell the story and place the pea on the bed. Ask a child to put a mattress on the bed and lay the princess on top. Tell the children that the princess does not look comfortable so they should add one more mattress. Continue adding 'one more' mattress until you reach the desired number or until the princess is comfortable. As each mattress is added, pose questions such as: *How many mattresses are there altogether? If we add one more, how many will there be?*
● You may then decide to reverse the process, taking away one mattress at a time and working out how many 'one less' will be.

### Learning objectives
**Calculating**
● Say the number that is one more than a given number. **(PSRN)**
**Early Learning Goal**
● Find one more or one less than a number from one to ten. **(PSRN)**

### Early mathematicians
begin to understand the concept of 'one more'.
**More confident mathematicians** understand that as they add 'one more' mattress the total number increases.

## Support and extension
● Limit the number of mattresses used to (say) five for younger children.
● Increase the number of mattresses for older children, encouraging them to add two at a time and work out 'two more' or 'two less'.

## Further activity
Enlarge photocopiable page 19 to A3. Colour, cut out and laminate (as separate pieces) the illustrations of the princess, mattresses, bed and pea. Stick Velcro to the back of each piece and onto a baseboard so that the children can build up their own princess's bed. Provide wipeable pens for the children to write the appropriate number on the mattresses as they add one more.

## Play link
Provide a dressing-up box containing clothes, crowns and shoes for princes and princesses, pieces of foam or cushions to represent the mattresses and wooden beads to represent peas. **(CD)**

## Home link
Suggest that parents or carers ask their children to count items around the home and say how many 'one more' would be.

### Cross-curricular links
**Language for Thinking**
● Use talk to connect ideas, explain what is happening and anticipate what might happen next. **(CLL)**
**Early Learning Goal**
● Use talk to organise, sequence and clarify thinking, ideas, feelings and events. **(CLL)**

# The Princess and the Pea

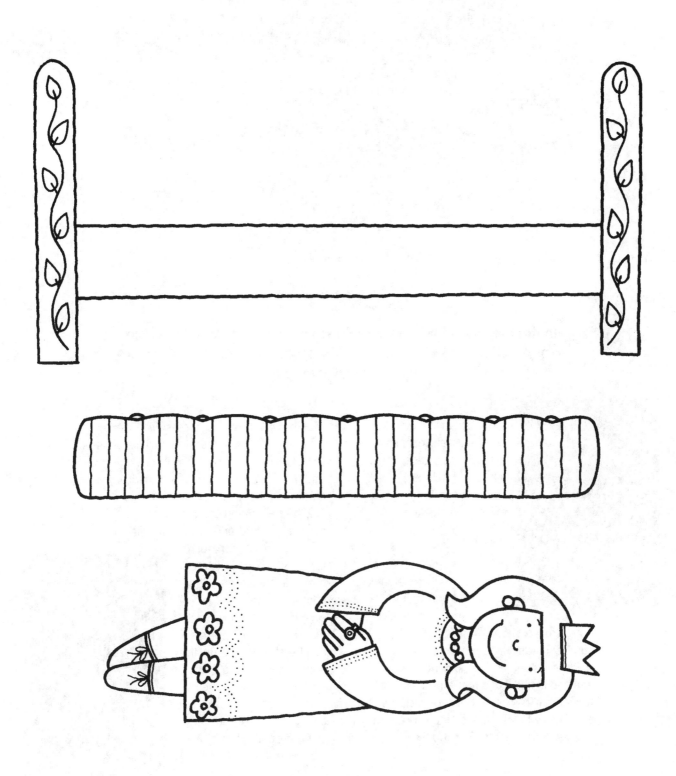

**SCHOLASTIC**
www.scholastic.co.uk

# Blast off!

**In this role-play activity, children discover a rocket and take on the roles of space-station workers as they count down to blast off before zooming away into space.**

**Early mathematicians** join in number rhymes and songs involving counting back. They begin to recognise the numerals 1 to 5 on cards and the computer keyboard.
**More confident mathematicians** order number cards 10 to 0 as they count back ready for take off.

## What you need

Large boxes to create a simple rocket; set of large 0 to 10 number cards; 'space' outfits and helmets; battery-operated microphone (optional).

## What to do

● Set the scene outside or in an open space before the children arrive, by making the boxes into a simple rocket shape and scattering the number cards on the ground. Gather the children around and explain that you were amazed to find that a rocket had landed. Ask them if they have ever seen pictures of a rocket taking off. How do the spacemen know when to set off? Talk about counting down from 10 to 0 for blast off.
● Look at the cards on the floor and tell the children that you think they are the countdown cards – a space-station worker must have dropped them! He will need the children's help. Give out the space outfits and appoint one child as the countdown officer and the others as space workers. Ask the space workers to pick up a countdown card and try to identify the numeral on it. When each child has a card, help them arrange themselves into a countdown line.
● Give the countdown officer a microphone so that he/she can call out the numbers from 10 to 0 as each child holds up their card in turn. As he/she calls out 'Blast off!' the children zoom off into space in all directions. On their return to Earth, gather

### Learning objectives
**Numbers as Labels and for Counting**
● Recognise numerals 1 to 5. **(PSRN)**
● Use some number names accurately in play. **(PSRN)**
**Early Learning Goals**
● Recognise numerals 1 to 9. **(PSRN)**
● Say and use number names in order in familiar contexts. **(PSRN)**

the children around the rocket again, appoint a new countdown officer, collect up the cards and pretend to accidentally drop them. The children then repeat the process as they prepare for launching a second time.

### Support and extension

● Encourage younger children to join in with number rhymes and songs that involve counting down from 5. Use a set of cards with numerals 5 to 0 during the rocket activity.

● Provide older children with a microphone and sets of smaller cards with numerals 10 to 0 to make their own countdown lines.

### Further activities

● Tell the children that you want them to help the countdown officer by writing down the count down numbers for him keep. Help younger children find the numerals 5 to 0 on the computer keyboard and print their work. Challenge older children to list and print the numbers 10 to 0 themselves.

● Share rocket stories with the children, such as *Rocket Countdown* by Nick Sharratt (Walker Books) that includes counting back

from 10, or *Whatever Next!* by Jill Murphy (Macmillan Children's Books) where Baby Bear goes to the moon in a cardboard box rocket.

### Play link

Provide a set of 0 to 5 cards, coloured play dough, paper plates, googly eyes or beads, coloured matchsticks and pipe cleaners. Sing the song:

Five little men in a flying saucer
Flew round the earth one day
They looked left and right,
but didn't like the sight
So one man flew away.

Ask the children to make their own play dough aliens and label the number of aliens on each paper plate or 'flying saucer'. **(CD)**

### Home link

Encourage parents to play counting-back games with their children, such as counting down how long it takes to wash their face, put on their socks or tidy their toys.

# How many biscuits?

**After making and decorating some tasty biscuits, children solve simple problems involving addition before they tuck in to what they have made.**

## What you need

Photocopiable page 23; biscuit recipe, equipment and ingredients needed to make plain biscuits; glacé cherries; raisins; chocolate chips; paper plates.

## What to do

● Check for food allergies or special dietary requirements before starting this activity. Tell the children that today they will be making biscuits to share at snack time. Read the 'What to make' card (from photocopiable page 23) together. Using the illustrations, count how many biscuits of each type they will be making. Then read the 'What to do' card together. Point out that the instructions are numbered, so the children must start with number 1. Use the illustrations to give clues.

● Make the biscuit dough and roll it out on a floured board. Look together at the 'What to make' card to see how many of each type of biscuit they will need. Cut out the biscuits and press cherries, chocolate chips or raisins on top of the appropriate number of biscuits. Ask the children to check that they have the correct number of each type of biscuit and count how many they have altogether.

● When the biscuits are cooked and have cooled, ask the children to wash their hands again before touching them. Encourage them to work out problems involving addition such as: *If you put the three cherry biscuits on a plate with two chocolate chip biscuits, how many will you have altogether?* Encourage the children to make up and solve simple problems of their own and then eat the biscuits.

### Early mathematicians
add up to five objects by counting the number of biscuits altogether.
### More confident mathematicians
add up to 10 biscuits, making up and solving their own addition problems.

### Learning objectives
**Calculating**
● Find the total number of items in two groups by counting all of them. **(PSRN)**
**Early Learning Goal**
● Begin to relate addition to combining two groups of objects and subtraction to 'taking away'. **(PSRN)**

## Support and extension

● Make just five large biscuits with younger children and involve them in counting and adding numbers to 5.
● Challenge older children to find their own ways of recording what they have done by drawing or making a tally.

## Further activity

Fill a bag with ten vegetables. Count the vegetables together and then sort them into their different types. Make up addition problems together, such as: *How many carrots and potatoes altogether?*

## Play link

Provide rolling pins, cutters, biscuit tin, play dough and large coloured beads to represent cherries, raisins and chocolate chips. Encourage the children to make and count a variety of play biscuits to fill the tin for a toys' picnic. **(PD)**

## Home link

Suggest that the children count and add things together at home, such as the forks and spoons on the table or tins of food in the cupboard.

### Cross-curricular links
**Reading**
● Know information can be relayed in the form of print. **(CLL)**
**Early Learning Goal**
● Show an understanding of how information can be found in non-fiction texts to answer questions about where, who, why and how. **(CLL)**

**22**

# How many biscuits?

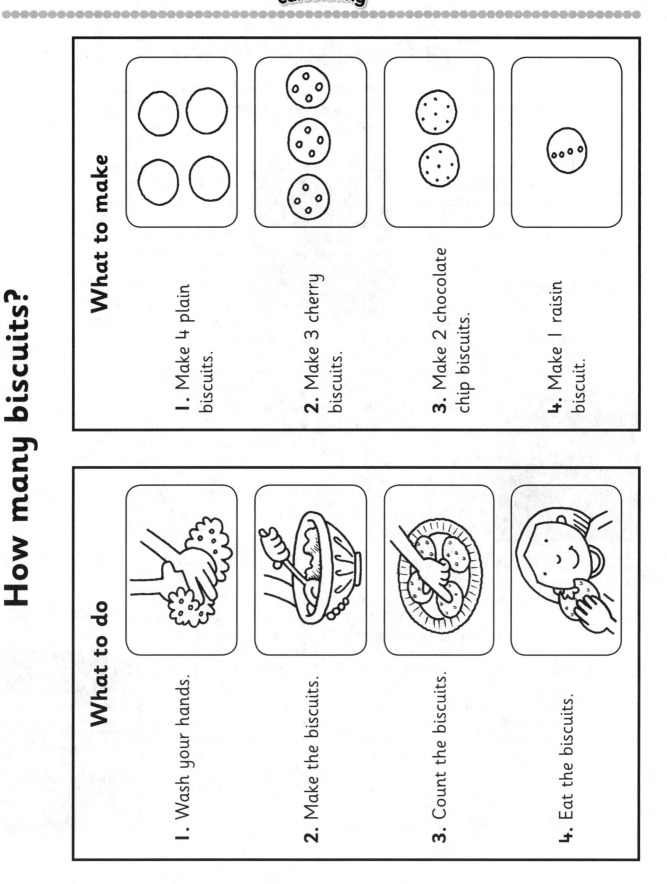

## What to make

1. Make 4 plain biscuits.

2. Make 3 cherry biscuits.

3. Make 2 chocolate chip biscuits.

4. Make 1 raisin biscuit.

## What to do

1. Wash your hands.

2. Make the biscuits.

3. Count the biscuits.

4. Eat the biscuits.

SCHOLASTIC
www.scholastic.co.uk

# The Queen of Hearts

**In this activity, children solve problems related to subtraction, based on the concept of the knave stealing the jam tarts in the nursery rhyme 'The Queen of Hearts'.**

## What you need
Laminated jam tart plates (see photocopiable page 25); paper crowns; cloak; red and white play dough; rolling pins; pastry cutters; bun tin.

## What to do
● Before the session, cut out and laminate the jam tart plate provided on photocopiable page 25.
● Teach the children the nursery rhyme 'The Queen of Hearts'. Tell them that they are going to pretend to be the King or Queen of Hearts and make some pretend jam tarts. Give them the crowns and aprons to wear as they make the jam tarts in a bun tin, rolling the play dough and using the pastry cutters. Make a blob of 'strawberry jam' in the middle of each one. Bake at a low heat until dried out.
● Choose one child to be the king or queen and wear a crown, and another child to be the knave and wear the cloak. Provide the king/queen with the laminated plate and ask him/her to place a jam tart on each circle on the plate. Count the number of tarts on the plate together. All of the children, except the knave, then cover their eyes, saying the rhyme together as the knave takes some of the tarts and runs away.
● When they open their eyes, the children work out how many tarts have gone by counting the empty circles. Help them make

### Learning objectives
**Calculating**
● Show an interest in number problems. **(PSRN)**
**Early Learning Goal**
● Begin to relate subtraction to taking away. **(PSRN)**

### Early mathematicians
begin to solve simple problems involving subtraction.
### More confident mathematicians
solve problems involving subtraction and record what they have done in their own ways.

sense of what has happened and predict what could happen: *There were five tarts on the plate. The knave stole one tart. How many are left? If he took one more, how many would be left?*
● The knave then brings the tarts back and the activity is repeated with other children in the key roles.

## Support and extension
● Play alongside younger children, supporting them with the counting and working out.
● Challenge older children to record what happened in pictures or numbers.

## Further activity
Wearing crowns and clean aprons, help the children to make real jam tarts. Keep a close watch to make sure none are stolen and enjoy them for a treat at the castle.

## Play link
Encourage talk and role play by turning the home corner into a royal kitchen where the kings and queens can prepare a banquet. **(CLL)**

## Home link
Encourage parents or carers to include simple taking-away games at bath time, such as lining five ducks on the side of the bath: *When one falls in, how many are left?*

### Cross-curricular links
**Using Equipment and Materials**
● Manipulate materials to create a planned effect. **(PD)**
**Early Learning Goal**
● Handle malleable materials safely and with increasing control. **(PD)**

# How many are left?

SCHOLASTIC
www.scholastic.co.uk

# Shape, space and measures

## Little Bo Peep

**In this activity, children help Little Bo Peep's sheep find their way back to her, describing their journey over, under and around obstacles.**

### What you need
Photocopiable page 27; outdoor play equipment; digital camera.

### What to do
● Before the session, photocopy, cut out and laminate the figures of Little Bo Peep and the sheep provided on photocopiable page 27. Hide the 'sheep' outside. Place various objects outside that the children can later safely journey under, over, through and around. These might include a table, slide and tunnel.
● Teach the children the nursery rhyme 'Little Bo Peep' and show them the cut-out figure, explaining that five of her sheep are lost. Go outside with the children and ask them to help you place Bo Peep where she can keep a look out for her sheep. Choose a vantage point together. Ask the children to help you find the sheep.
● When the sheep are all found, give each child a sheep to look after. Lead the children on their journey back to Bo Peep, encouraging them to describe what they are doing – for example, going around the tree, past the gate and under the table. At each obstacle, take a digital photograph showing the children manoeuvring the sheep on their journey until they are reunited with Bo Peep.
● Print or make a slide show of the photographs.

### Support and extension
● Help younger children to use the correct words to describe position.
● Encourage older children to plan their own journeys and recount their adventure when they look at the photographs.

### Further activity
Create a farm using boxes for buildings, fabric for fields and twigs pushed into Plasticine® for trees. Press the sheep into pieces of Plasticine® and help the children to hide and find them by giving positional clues.

### Play link
Provide a selection of nursery rhymes in different media for the children to enjoy. **(CLL)**

### Home link
Suggest that parents or carers visit the library and choose a nursery rhyme book to share.

> **Early mathematicians** enjoy manoeuvring the sheep and begin to use positional language. **More confident mathematicians** use positional language accurately as they look at photographs and recount their journeys.

> **Learning objectives**
> **Shape, Space and Measures**
> ● Observe and use positional language. **(PSRN)**
> ● Find items from positional or directional clues. **(PSRN)**
> **Early Learning Goal**
> ● Use everyday words to describe position. **(PSRN)**

> **Cross-curricular links**
> **Dispositions and Attitudes**
> ● Show confidence in linking up with others for support and guidance. **(PSED)**
> **Early Learning Goal**
> ● Be confident to try new activities, initiate ideas and speak in a familiar group. **(PSED)**

# Little Bo Peep

# Walking like a robot

**Children enjoy moving like robots and give instructions to make an adult 'robot' move. They use directional language as they use remote-controlled vehicles.**

## What you need

A battery-operated toy robot, if available (or pictures of robots); a selection of remote-controlled vehicles.

## What to do

● Show the children a robot (or if this is not possible, show pictures of robots). Talk about the way that the robot moves stiffly and demonstrate how to move like a robot. Ask the children to follow you around the room, walking like robots.
● Gather the children together and teach them the words of the poem 'I Am A Robot' (by Janet Perry).

### I Am A Robot

I am a robot. Watch me walk.
Listen to the way I like to talk.

My feet are big and heavy.

My arms are stiff and slow.
I am a robot. Watch me walk.
Listen to the way I like to talk.

My head can turn from side to side.
My eyes are wobbly and open wide.
I am a robot. Watch me walk.
Listen to the way I like to talk.

My hands and elbows jerk around.
I can wiggle my ears without a sound.
I am a robot. Watch me walk.
Listen to the way I like to talk.

● Say the poem together, moving the appropriate parts of the body, as you walk about like the robot.
● Explain to the children

that robots cannot think for themselves – they need some instructions. Tell the children that you are going to pretend to be a robot. Enlist the help of another adult, who will stand behind you and model how to call out instructions to control the robot. Keep the instructions simple, such as *forwards, backwards, stop, left* and *right*. Take extra time helping children understand *left* and *right*. Encourage them to take turns in giving you instructions or in being the robot themselves. Older children can work with a partner, taking turns to be the robot or calling out the instructions.

● Show the children a remote-controlled car with very simple controls. Explain that the car needs instructions just as the robot did. Talk about the symbols used for the different commands. Ask the children to work out how to control the car to go forwards, backwards and turn left or right. Give them time to experiment freely in manoeuvring the car around the room or outside.

## Support and extension

● Support younger children in understanding directional language and using a remote-controlled vehicle.
● Challenge older children to control the car on its journey from one side of the room to its garage on the other.

## Further activities

● Ask the children to help you use cones or markers to create a simple roadway outside. Draw a house at one end and place the sand and water trays at the other end to represent the seaside. Encourage the children to work with a partner as one directs the other from home to the seaside.
● Provide simple programmable floor robots. Support the children in using directional language as they experiment in controlling the robots.

## Play link

Provide a collection of boxes, packets, cardboard tubes, sticky tape and scissors so that the children can create their own robots. Use these to create a display and to encourage the children to talk about the 3D shapes they have used. **(CD)**

## Home links

Suggest that parents or carers include their children when using the controls on a television or music player.

### Cross-curricular links
**ICT**
● Use ICT to perform simple functions, such as selecting a channel on the TV remote control. **(KUW)**
**Early Learning Goal**
● Find out about and identify the uses of everyday technology and use information and communication technology and programmable toys to support their learning. **(KUW)**

# Spots, stripes and more

**Introduce children to pattern through a lively story, in which the mum and dad only wear spotty and stripy clothes.**

## What you need

A copy of *My Mum and Dad Make Me Laugh* by Nick Sharratt (Walker Books); clothes rail (if available); patterned clothes; lengths of patterned fabric; photocopiable page 31.

## What to do

● Before the session, enlarge photocopiable page 31 to A3, and laminate.

● Share the story *My Mum and Dad Make Me Laugh* with the children, talking about the types of patterns the characters in the story liked to wear and picking out all the spotty and stripy items in the illustrations. Ask the children to bring in their own patterned clothes for everyone to look at. Display these on a clothes rail, if available.

● When you have gathered a variety of patterned clothes, share the story again and show the children the collection. Encourage them to talk about the different patterns and colours and say which they like, giving reasons. Encourage them to try on the clothes and wrap themselves in the patterned fabric.

● Ask the children to look carefully at the patterns and sort the clothes and fabric into piles – for example, putting all the stripy things or all the spotty things together. Encourage them to trace over the patterns with their fingers.

● Show the children the laminated pattern squares. Talk about the patterns and

**Learning objectives**
**Shape, Space and Measures**
● Use familiar objects and common shapes to create and recreate patterns.
**Early Learning Goal**
● Talk about, recognise and recreate simple patterns. **(PSRN)**

**Early mathematicians** begin to notice pattern in everyday items and make patterns of their own.
**More confident mathematicians** notice similarities and differences between patterns and create their own patterns.

shapes using language such as straight, zigzag, wavy or spirals to describe the patterns and shapes. Encourage the children to use finger paints to trace over the patterns on the laminated cards or to use the cards for ideas and create their own patterns on paper.

## Support and extension

● Support younger children by using simple describing words when talking about the patterns.

● Extend the activity by encouraging pairs of children wearing the patterned clothes to describe their outfits to each other.

## Further activity

Set up an area outside with lengths of lining paper, paints, rollers, printing stampers and shapes. Challenge the children to print patterned wallpaper for the role-play or reading area.

## Play link

Fill a box with spotty or stripy fabrics or papers for children to examine. Provide strips of coloured paper and coloured counters for children to create their own patterns. **(KUW)**

## Home link

Suggest that the children look around their homes for patterns on kitchenware, duvet covers, curtains and tablecloths.

**Cross-curricular links**
**Exploration and Investigation**
● Notice and comment on patterns. **(KUW)**
**Early Learning Goal**
● Look closely at similarities, differences, patterns and change. **(KUW)**

# Spots, stripes and more

www.scholastic.co.uk

# All about shapes

**Children look for and explore 2D shapes in the environment and through playing outdoor games, before creating their own shapes using a paint program on the computer.**

**Early mathematicians** show interest in shapes and begin to name them. They create shapes, with help, when using a paint program on the computer.
**More confident mathematicians** begin to describe shapes and work independently to create their own shapes using a paint program.

## What you need

Chalk or markers; computer and simple drawing program; printer; A4 paper; sequins; glue.

## What to do

● Over a few weeks spend some time as shape detectives, looking for and talking about shapes in the environment in and around the setting. Encourage the children to record the shapes they see in their own ways – these could include drawings, photographs or pictures.
● To help the children understand the concept of shapes and their properties, play outdoor games that incorporate shapes, such as circle or parachute games. Draw large circles, triangles, squares and rectangles on the play area or outline the shapes using markers so that the children can include the shapes into their play. Encourage them to play follow-my-leader games with you around the shapes – for example, jump round and round the circle; hop along the straight line; tiptoe round the corner, and so on. Give instructions such as *Run to the triangle! Stand next to a square!* or *Sit inside a circle!*
● When the children are familiar with shapes, show them how to use a simple drawing program on the computer to create their own shapes. Name the shapes and talk about

### Learning objectives
**Shape, Space and Measures**
● Show awareness of similarities in shapes in the environment. **(PSRN)**
● Begin to use mathematical names for 'solid' 3D shapes and 'flat' 2D shapes and mathematical terms to describe shapes. **(PSRN)**
**Early Learning Goal**
● Use language such as 'circle' or 'bigger' to describe the shape and size of solid and flat shapes. **(PSRN)**

their properties, counting the sides and corners. Ask the children to draw three or four shapes and use the flood fill tool to fill them with colour. Help the children print their work and cut around each shape. Invite them to decorate the shapes using sequins. Laminate and cut out the shapes. Attach brightly coloured wool to the shapes and hang them to make mobiles for the setting.

### Support and extension
● Make sure that younger children understand the language associated with shapes and support them in using the paint program.
● Encourage older children to work more independently when using the computer, describing each shape as they draw it.

### Further activities
● Challenge the children to use a paint program on the computer to make a simple pattern using mathematical shapes and the flood fill tool. Print the designs and mount them close together to create one large piece of art work.
● Present the children with a collection of empty boxes, tubes and packets. Challenge them to find circles, squares, rectangles and triangles on the faces of the boxes. Explain to them that you need somewhere to store these boxes and ask them to use sponge dabbers to print mathematical shapes on the sides of a large cardboard box to make a container.

### Play link
Provide a selection of large coloured shapes cut out of card and a collection of collage materials such as 'googly' eyes, matchsticks, lollipop sticks, buttons and card. Encourage the children to make the card shapes into shape people or animals and display them pegged to a washing line. **(CD)**

### Home link
Give each child a shape to take home and ask them to search for similar shapes around their home.

### Cross-curricular links
**ICT**
● Complete a simple program on the computer. **(KUW)**
**Early Learning Goal**
● Find out about and identify the uses of everyday technology and use information communication technology and programmable toys to support their learning. **(KUW)**

# Make it match

In this activity, children are introduced to symmetry as they press blobs of paint between their hands or make a giant-sized picture outdoors.

## What you need
Finger paint; pictures of butterflies; chalk; equipment such as hoops, beanbags, balls and quoits; water pots; large paintbrushes.

## What to do
● Paint blobs of finger paint on the palm of one hand, press your hands together and then place them side by side with the palms uppermost. Ask the children what they notice. Encourage them to make their own symmetrical patterns on their hands.

● Gather the children together and show them the pictures of butterflies. Focus on the patterns and colours, pointing out that the wings 'match' each other. Use chalk to draw a very large symmetrical outline of a butterfly on a hard play surface outside. Ask the children to decorate the wings by placing items such as balls, hoops, beanbags and quoits on them, trying to make the wings match each other.
● Give the children pots of water and household paintbrushes to draw their own butterflies on the play surface, decorating them with the play equipment.

## Support and extension
● Spend extra time with younger children looking for, and talking about, symmetrical patterns in and around the setting.

> **Early mathematicians** begin to be aware of symmetry as they look for patterns and pictures where both sides 'match'. **More confident mathematicians** try out their own ideas to make symmetrical patterns and pictures.

> **Learning objectives**
> **Shape, Space and Measures**
> ● Show awareness of symmetry. **(PSRN)**
> ● Use own methods to work through a problem. **(PSRN)**
> **Early Learning Goal**
> ● Use developing mathematical ideas and methods to solve practical problems. **(PSRN)**

● Provide paints, paper and collage materials for older children to experiment in making their own symmetrical pictures or patterns.

## Further activity
Enlarge photocopiable page 35 to A3. Together with the children, look at the outline of a castle featured on the sheet. Identify the 2D shapes together and ask the children to tell you if the two sides of the castle 'match' each other. Model how to paint the two halves to match each other and challenge the children to paint their own castles in a similar way. When the pictures are dry, cut the castles along the lines of symmetry, mix up the pieces and ask the children to find the matching pieces.

## Play link
Provide strips of large-squared paper (two squares wide) with the central line drawn thickly with a black marker pen. Ask the children to use items such as coloured cotton reels, buttons or coloured bricks to make patterns that match either side of the line. **(KUW)**

## Home link
Suggest that parents or carers help their children look out for and talk about patterns they see on the way to and from the setting – for example, in houses, windows, grates and bricks.

> **Cross-curricular links**
> **Exploration and investigation**
> ● Notice and comment on patterns. **(KUW)**
> **Early Learning Goal**
> ● Look closely at similarities, differences, patterns and change. **(KUW)**

# Make it match

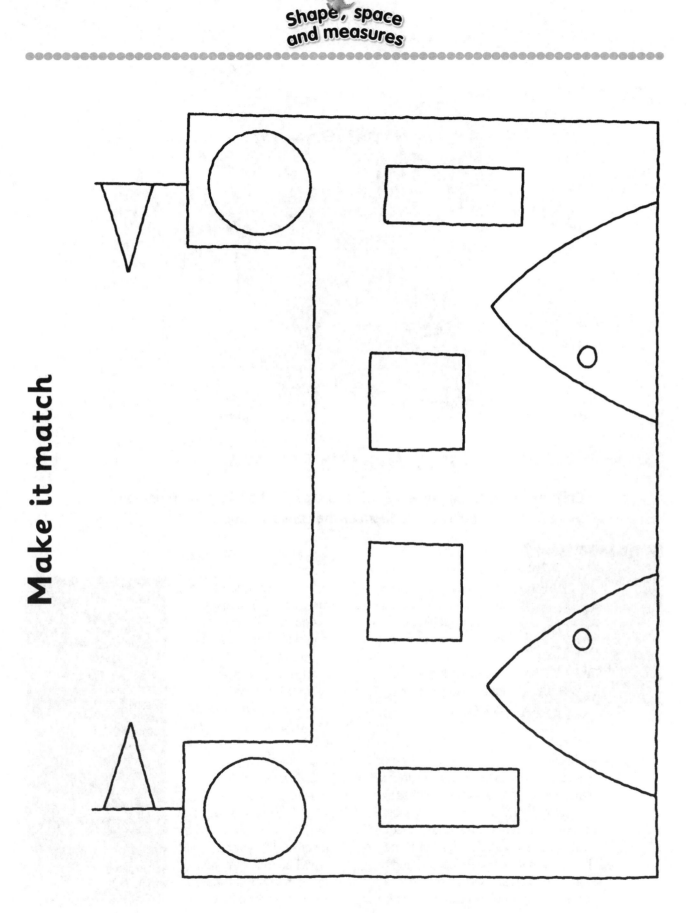

SCHOLASTIC
www.scholastic.co.uk

# Building a house

**Children discover the properties of 3D shapes by handling them and even going inside them as they build a house.**

**Early mathematicians** become aware of the differences between 3D shapes as they use them in building.

**More confident mathematicians** describe the properties of shapes and begin to use their correct mathematical names.

## What you need

Assorted cardboard boxes and tubes of all shapes and sizes (including at least one giant-sized box, such as those used to hold large electrical appliances); glue, sticky tape; assorted 'shape' sponges; paint.

## What to do

● Choose a reason for the children to build a house. This could be as part of a theme about houses or to represent a house in a story such as one of the Three Little Pigs' houses or the Three Bears' house. Clear a large space (or work outside). Talk to the children about the house you want them to make and discuss what it should look like. Show them the boxes and ask which

one would be most suitable to use for the house.

● Cut a door shape in the largest box, leaving the 'hinge' so that it will open and close. Encourage the children to go inside the box and experience what it is like to be inside the shape. Ask them to touch the walls and tell you if they are flat or curved and to count the sides.

● Gather the children together and ask them what they need to add to the box to make it look like a house. If they want to add a pitched roof, help them make this from cardboard. They could use a box and

### Learning objectives
**Shape, Space and Measures**

● Show curiosity about and observation of shapes by talking about how they are the same or why some are different. **(PSRN)**

● Begin to use mathematical names for 'solid' 3D shapes and 'flat' 2D shapes and mathematical terms to describe shapes. **(PSRN)**

**Early Learning Goal**

● Use language such as 'circle' or 'bigger; to describe the shape and size of solids and flat shapes. **(PSRN)**

cardboard tube to make a chimney, a long tube to make a drainpipe and glue on rectangles of paper to make windows. As the children handle the boxes and tubes, encourage them to find out more about their properties by seeing if the shapes will roll or stack, or by counting the sides and corners. Introduce the mathematical names for shapes as you think appropriate.

● Provide paint and circle-, triangle- and rectangle-shaped sponges so that the children can choose which ones to use to print 2D shapes on the sides of the house.

## Support and extension

● Help younger children to feel the differences between the shapes and extend their language using terms such as flat, curved, round and corners.

● Use the correct mathematical names for 2D and 3D shapes with older children.

## Further activities

● If there is building work being carried out in your area, visit the site (keeping at a safe distance behind the barriers) so that the children can see building at first hand. Back

in the setting, encourage them to refer to books and pictures of buildings as they use construction kits or large building bricks to make their own buildings, talking about the shapes as they do so.

● Provide additional resources so that the children can incorporate the house into their imaginative or role play. If, for example, it is the Three Bears' house, you could add dressing-up clothes for Goldilocks, masks for the three bears, porridge bowls and spoons, different-sized chairs and cushions for beds.

## Play link

Provide a variety of boxes and tubes, scissors and sticky tape and encourage children to explore the properties of the shapes as they make their own models. **(PD)**

## Home link

Suggest that parents or carers play a game of 'I Spy shapes' with their children on their way to the setting.

**Cross-curricular links**
**Exploring Media and Materials**
● Create 3D structures. **(CD)**
**Early Learning Goal**
● Explore colour, texture, shape, form and space in two or three dimensions. **(CD)**

# The messy princess

In this activity, children discover a jewellery box filled with a tangle of necklaces. They sort the necklaces, discovering that they are all different lengths.

**Early mathematicians** sort through the necklaces with adult support as they work out which are the longest and shortest.
**More confident mathematicians** begin to develop their own methods as they compare and sort the necklaces according to their length.

## What you need

An attractive box; a selection of beaded necklaces of varying lengths, colours and patterns; ruler or dowelling.

## What to do

● Gather the children together and show them the box. Explain that it belongs to a messy princess who never tidies things away. The princess has lots of beautiful jewels and necklaces, but she just drops them into her jewellery box and they become tangled. Build up the children's anticipation and open the box with some drama to reveal the tangle of necklaces.
● Tell the children that you want them to

help the princess by sorting out the jewellery box for her. Help them untangle the necklaces and ask each child in turn to choose a necklace and lay it on the table, with one end touching the end of the table. Make sure they are laid in straight lines. Talk about each necklace, discussing the colour, shape and size of the beads. Encourage the children to look for patterns in the way the beads are threaded.

● As each necklace is laid on the table, encourage discussion by asking questions about length such as: *Is your necklace longer or shorter than Toby's? Which is the longest? Which is the shortest? Are two necklaces the same length?* Ask the

### Learning objectives
**Shape, Space and Measures**
● Order two or three items by length or height. **(PSRN)**
**Early Learning Goal**
● Use developing mathematical ideas and methods to solve practical problems. **(PSRN)**

children to remember which is the longest and which is the shortest.

● Show the children how to fasten the necklaces and then slip them onto a ruler or piece of dowelling. Hold the ruler horizontally and ask the children to look again. Do the necklaces look longer or shorter now? Is the longest one still the longest? Encourage the children to try on the necklaces, looking at themselves in a mirror as they compare them.

### Support and extension
● Use a smaller number of necklaces when younger children are sorting and make sure that the difference in their lengths is obvious.
● Present older children with the jewellery box and challenge them to choose their own way to sort the necklaces from the longest to the shortest.

### Further activities
● Tell the children that the princess is going to a party and she would like a special, new necklace to wear, but she has not decided whether to wear a long necklace or a short one. Ask each child to help her decide by making her a selection of long and short necklaces using laces, large

beads or coloured cotton reels.
● Provide a washing basket containing several of the princess' scarves. Ask the children to help her by washing the scarves and pegging them on the line. While they are drying, ask the children to find the longest and shortest scarves, or ask older children to arrange them in order of length.

### Play link
Show the children a box of hair ribbons of different lengths that belong to the princess. Explain that you want them to pretend to be her younger brother or sister who thinks the ribbons are playthings and takes the box and ties each one along a fence, railing or gate. When they are hanging in a line, talk with the children about the differences in length. **(PSRN)**

### Home link
Suggest that parents encourage their children to compare lengths of everyday things at home – for example, sorting spoons into long ones and short ones or asking: *Whose trousers are the longest? Which sock is the shortest?*

# Heavier or lighter?

**Children compare the weights of bucketfuls of pebbles, sand and bark as they make roads for their lorries, tractors and diggers.**

**Early mathematicians** experience holding and carrying a variety of materials and deciding which is heavier or lighter.
**More confident mathematicians** solve problems involving the understanding of weighing and order items by weight.

## What you need

Heaps of washed pebbles, play sand and compost; buckets; spades; a wheelbarrow; toy lorries, tractors and diggers; hard hats and fluorescent vests, if available.

## What to do

● Check for any allergies before starting this outdoor activity. Show the children the heaps of pebbles, compost and play sand. Explain that you want them to be road builders and use these materials to make roads wide enough for the lorries, tractors and diggers. Give each child a hard hat and fluorescent vest, if available. Encourage the children to handle the materials, talking about their texture, colour and smell. Ask them to take

a big handful of each material. Does a handful of pebbles feel heavier or lighter than a handful of compost?
● Explain to the children that they can fill the buckets or wheelbarrow with the materials using their hands or the spades and transport them to the area where you want them to make the roads. Remind them to use the equipment and materials safely and ask them why they should not fill up the wheelbarrow with pebbles or sand. If they do not realise it would be too heavy to move, demonstrate this. Help the children make tracks wide enough for the vehicles to run along. Encourage them to compare the width of the road and the width of the vehicles.

## Learning objectives
**Shape, Space and Measures**
● Order two items by weight or capacity. **(PSRN)**
**Early Learning Goal**
● Use language such as 'greater', 'smaller', 'heavier' or 'lighter' to compare quantities. **(PSRN)**

● As the children are working, ask questions to encourage their understanding of weighing and the use of language associated with measuring weight. For example: *Which bucket is heavier? Is the bucket of pebbles lighter than the bucket of compost? Is the big bucket of sand heavier than the small bucket of sand?*

## Support and extension
● Help younger children to 'weigh' items held in their hands or in buckets, deciding which is heavier.
● Challenge older children to solve problems such as: *Can you put stones into three buckets and say which one is heavy, heavier and the heaviest? Can you fill two buckets to weigh about the same?*

## Further activities
● Put sturdy balances outside and show the children how they can put items such as stones in one pan and sand in the other and see which is heavier. Alternatively, ask them to add more to the lighter side until both sides weigh about the same.

● Interest the children in finding out about large vehicles by filling a small wheelbarrow with information books and pictures (from catalogues) about lorries, tractors and diggers. Also include paper, crayons, scissors and glue to encourage the children to make or draw vehicles.

## Play link
Cover a safe outside area with play sand and provide large diggers, lorries and tractors. Encourage the children to run the vehicles over the sand, making tracks and comparing the patterns. **(KUW)**

## Home link
Suggest that parents and carers let their children help put away the grocery shopping, commenting on the weight of packets or tins, noticing which is heavier or lighter.

### Cross-curricular links
**Exploration and Investigation**
● Show understanding of cause/effect relations. **(KUW)**
**Dispositions and Attitudes**
● Display high levels of involvement in activities. **(PSED)**
**Early Learning Goals**
● Ask questions about why things happen and how things work. **(KUW)**
● Continue to be interested, excited and motivated to learn. **(PSED)**

Shape, space
and measures

# Firefighters

**In this role-play activity, children help to solve a problem for the firefighters as they fill buckets to find out which one holds the most water.**

**Early mathematicians** begin to understand the concepts of empty, full and half full, when filling buckets with water.
**More confident mathematicians** work out ways to find which bucket holds the most water.

## What you need
Water tray; two buckets of different sizes; plastic jug; firefighters' helmets and outfits if available; ride-on play vehicle; lengths of hosepipe.

## What to do
● Work outside for this activity. Tell the children that today they are going to be firefighters for the day. Give each child a helmet and firefighter's outfit, if available. Explain that the firefighters want to buy some new water buckets and must decide which ones to buy. They would like the children to help and have sent two buckets for them to try out as they want to buy the one that holds the most water. Show the children the buckets, water tray and plastic jug and explain that the firefighters have asked them to solve the problem.

● Which bucket do the children think will hold the most water? How can they find out? Can they use the jug to help them solve the problem? How many jugfuls of water do they think it will take to fill each bucket? Talk about the fact that the jug must be full each time they measure the water and encourage the use of language such as full, half full and empty. Count with the children as they fill the bucket and either keep a tally on a whiteboard or write the number of jugfuls needed. Look at the second bucket together. Is it bigger or smaller than the first? How many jugfuls of water do they think will be needed to fill it? Repeat the measuring process.
● Talk to the children and ask questions about their findings: *Which bucket held the most jugfuls of water? Which is the biggest*

### Learning objectives
**Shape, Space and Measures**
● Order two items by weight or capacity.
**(PSRN)**
**Early Learning Goal**
● Use language such as 'greater', 'smaller', 'heavier' or 'lighter' to compare quantities.
**(PSRN)**

*bucket?* Label the biggest bucket ready for the firefighters. Encourage the children to stay in role and use the ride-on vehicle as a fire engine and the buckets and hoses to put out pretend fires.

### Support and extension
● Support younger children in understanding the concepts of full, half full and empty. Encourage them to count with you as they fill the buckets with jugfuls of water.
● Ask older children if they can think of any other ways to find out which bucket holds the most water.

### Further activities
● Provide a buckets and damp sand in a tray or sandpit. Encourage the children to talk about what they find out as they fill the buckets and make sandcastles. Ask questions such as: *Which bucket makes the biggest sandcastle? Can you half-fill all of the buckets? How many small bucketfuls do you need to fill the big bucket?*
● Make holes in several buckets. Tell the

children that the firefighters have asked for help again as all of their buckets have holes in them and they have no money left to buy new ones. Ask the children to fill the buckets with water and see what happens. Challenge them to help by mending the holes to stop the water running out. Provide materials for them to use such as parcel tape, Blu-Tack, paper, waxed paper and plastic.

### Play link
Provide assorted containers in the water tray, with and without holes in them, to encourage experimenting and measuring activities. **(PSRN)**

### Home link
Suggest that parents or carers include a variety of clean, safe plastic containers at bath time to encourage their children to experiment in filling and emptying them.

### Cross-curricular links
**Language for Thinking**
● Use talk to connect ideas, explain what is happening and anticipate what might happen next. **(CLL)**
**Early Learning Goal**
● Use talk to organise, sequence and clarify thinking, ideas and feelings. **(CLL)**

# Rock around the clock!

**Children order events in their day, dance to the song 'Rock around the clock' and identify numerals on a giant-sized outdoor clock.**

**Early mathematicians** begin to be aware of the order of significant events in their daily routine and recognise some numerals on a clock face. **More confident mathematicians** begin to relate events to specific times and recognise the numerals on a clock face.

## What you need

A recording of the song 'Rock around the clock'; a large clock face; large 1 to 12 number cards; 12 markers or cones.

## What to do

● Talk to the children about times that are significant to them each day, such as breakfast time, dinner time, bath time and so on. Encourage discussion about which times they enjoy most, and why. Ask the children if they know of any particular times during the day, such as 12 o'clock is dinner time. Make a point of mentioning one or two key times over the following weeks, such as: *It's 10 o'clock – time for our snack or It's 3 o'clock – time to go home.*
● Explain that when we want to know the time we look at a clock or watch. Show the children a large clock face and ask

them if they recognise any of the numerals. Read these together.
● Gather a group of children together inside or outside and play a recording of 'Rock around the clock', inviting the children to dance along with you. Stop them and ask them to listen for the words 'One o'clock, two o'clock, three o'clock, rock' and so on, then continue dancing and singing.
● Tell the children that you want them to help you make a giant clock outside. Place cones or markers where each number should be and put the appropriate number card next to it. Invite the children to follow you in a line around the outside of the clock, with the children chanting:

One o'clock, two o'clock, three o'clock, rock.
What is the time on this clock?

**Learning objectives**
**Numbers as Labels and for Counting**
● Recognise numerals 1 to 5, then 1 to 9. **(PSRN)**
● Use everyday language related to time; order and sequence familiar events. **(PSRN)**
**Early Learning Goal**
● Recognise numerals 1 to 9. **(PSRN)**

# Shape, space and measures

● Call out 'o'clock' times or a special time such as *It's 10 o'clock… snack time!* The children then run around the outside of the clock and stand next to the appropriate number.

## Support and extension
● When playing the clock game with younger children, focus on recognising numerals 1 to 5.
● Provide older children with very large circles of paper and challenge them to paint the numbers to make an outdoor giant's clock.

## Further activities
● Ask the children to choose items to represent key times in the day, such as a bowl and spoon for breakfast time, a lunch box for dinner time, a knife and fork for tea time, a sponge for bath time and a teddy bear for bed time. Talk about the first thing that happens each day, what happens next and so on, putting the items in a line in the correct order.
● Encourage the children to talk about

things from their past that have special meaning for them, such as birthdays. Begin to put birthdays in order saying: *First you were one, then you were two, then you were three, now you are four,* showing the corresponding numerals.

## Play link
Provide a collection of picture books to share, with time as their theme, such as *What's the Time, Mr Wolf?* by Colin Hawkins (Egmont Books) or *Spot Tells the Time* by Eric Hill (Putnam Publishing). Play the game 'What's the Time, Mr Wolf?' with the children. **(CLL)**

## Home link
Encourage parents or carers to talk with their children about their daily routines, beginning to refer to the time. For example: *It's 7 o'clock – time for bed.*

### Cross-curricular links
**Time**
● Remember and talk about significant events in their own experience. **(KUW)**
● Begin to differentiate between past and present. **(KUW)**
**Early Learning Goal**
● Find out about past and present events in their own lives, and in those of their families and other people they know. **(KUW)**

# Open the box!

## The gardener's box

Children open the gardener's box and have fun solving problems that involve planting seeds, recognising numerals and counting.

### What you need

A box containing: four small plant pots; eight untreated bean seeds; a bag of compost; two children's trowels and one small watering can. Also needed: photocopiable page 47, enlarged to A3 and the contents card, instructions cards and badges laminated separately; safety pins taped to the back of the badges.

### Learning objectives

**Numbers as Labels and for Counting**
● Recognise numerals 1 to 5. **(PSRN)**
● Count up to three or four objects by saying one number name for each item. **(PSRN)**
● Begin to count beyond ten. **(PSRN)**
**Early Learning Goals**
● Recognise numerals 1 to 9. **(PSRN)**
● Count reliably up to ten everyday objects. **(PSRN)**
● Use developing mathematical ideas to solve practical problems. **(PSRN)**

### What to do

● Ask the children to guess what is inside the box. Challenge them to look inside for clues telling them what to do. Give each child a gardener's badge to wear.
● Invite the children to read the contents card with you, recognising the numerals, counting the items in the box and checking there is the correct number of each. Show them the instructions cards and ask them to help you put them in the right order by looking at the number on each one. Follow the instructions together, encouraging the children to use the picture cues to help them. When the beans are planted, ask the children to count how many they planted altogether, remembering there are two in each pot. Label the pots.
● Over the next few weeks encourage the children to watch as the plants grow, noticing which plant in their pot is taller, counting the leaves and making their own pictorial records.

### Support and extension

● Support younger children by modelling touching or moving items as you count them.
● Encourage older children to count in twos, fives and tens, by giving them a handful of beans and asking them to find different ways to count the beans.

### Further activity

When the beans begin to grow, ask the children to find a way to show how much the beans grow each week. Encourage discussion and try out their ideas. They could take photographs, draw pictures or make marks on a cane next to the plant.

### Play link

Share the story of 'Jack and the Beanstalk'. Fill a plant pot with the story book, a tape recording or CD of the story, paper, crayons and pencils to encourage speaking and listening, drawing and writing. **(CLL)**

### Home link

Suggest that parents or carers encourage their children to look at the wide range of packets of seeds available when visiting garden centres or shops.

### Cross-curricular links

**Exploration and Investigation**
● Show an awareness of change. **(KUW)**
**Early Learning Goal**
● Look closely at similarities, differences, patterns and change. **(KUW)**

# The gardener's box

## The gardener's box

4 plant pots

8 bean seeds

compost — compost

2 trowels

1 watering can

I am a gardener

I am a gardener

I am a gardener

I am a gardener

1. Put compost in the plant pot

2. Push 2 bean seeds in the compost.

3. Water the seeds.

4. Put the plant pot in the sun.

# The teacher's box

**Children sort and re-pack the contents of a teacher's box, using the opportunity to solve problems, count in ones and twos, and recognise numbers and 2D shapes.**

**Early mathematicians** enjoy joining in with counting rhymes and songs and begin to recognise numbers 1 to 5. **More confident mathematicians** count in twos, recognise 2D shapes and begin to record, in their own ways, what they have done.

## What you need

A box containing: photocopied, coloured and laminated 'pencils' (see photocopiable page 50); two of each coloured pencils; mathematical shape sponges; pot of paint; notebooks; pens; number rhyme books; number rhyme CDs or tapes. Also needed: CD or tape player; teacher's chair; table and chairs; whiteboard and pens.

## What to do

● Before the children arrive, set up a small role-play teaching area with the teacher's chair, children's table, chairs, CD or tape player, whiteboard and pens. Tip the items from the teacher's box onto the table.
● Show the children the jumble of items on the table, explaining that these are the things the teacher had prepared for the day, but you knocked over her box by accident and now they are all mixed up. Ask the children to help you sort the items, talking about and naming them as they do so.
● Ask the children to work together to check that all of the 'pencil cards' from 1 to 10 are there, by laying them on the table in the correct order and telling you which number comes next. Challenge the children to sort the real pencils by colour, estimate and then count how many there are altogether. To encourage counting in twos, ask: *Is there a quicker way to count the pencils?* Sort the shape sponges together, asking the children to name and count how many there are of

each shape. Ask: *What do you think the teacher wants the children to do with these sponges? Is the pot of paint a clue?*

● Tell the children that when they have sorted out the box they will be pretending to be the teacher and children in the school role-play area. Look through the books and CDs or tapes containing number rhymes and songs and ask the children if they know any that they could 'teach' the children when they are in the school role-play area. Encourage them to practise by teaching them to you first. Show them how to use the tape/CD player and then sing along with some of the rhymes.

● As the children pack the box, ask older children to make a checklist to record the items they put in it, using drawings or numbers. Begin the role play by choosing one child to be the teacher and the rest to be the pupils. Join in with the role play, encouraging problem solving and the development of mathematical language.

## Support and extension

● Support younger children by focusing on sorting activities, number rhymes and number recognition from 1 to 5.

● During the role play, encourage older children to record numbers or drawings, or to make tallies in their notepads.

## Further activities

● Using chalk, draw lines of footprints in sets of two on the hard play area to encourage the children to count the footprints in twos as they jump along.

● Encourage the children to make rows of prints using the shape sponges, counting the number of squares, triangles, circles and so on, that they make.

## Play link

Provide number rhyme books, number cards and a tape recorder to encourage the children to enjoy singing, recording and playing back number rhymes. **(KUW)**

## Home link

Encourage the children to learn a simple number rhyme and teach it to someone at home.

### Cross-curricular links
**ICT**
● Know how to operate simple equipment. **(KUW)**
**Early Learning Goal**
● Find out about and identify the uses of everyday technology and use ICT and programmable toys to support their learning. **(KUW)**

# The teacher's box

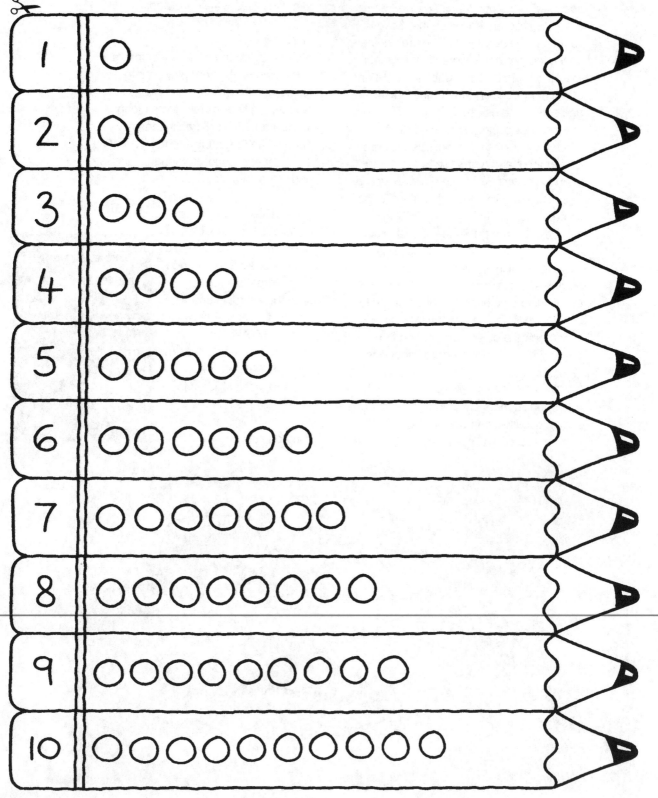

# The fantasy box

In this role-play activity, children find a fantasy box with magic wands and envelopes full of stars. This provides opportunities for addition and subtraction activities, as well as hopping, skipping and jumping games.

**Early mathematicians** sort and count large and small stars, finding the total by counting the whole group.
**More confident mathematicians** solve simple problems involving the addition and subtraction of stars.

## What you need

A special shiny box containing: a fairy skirt and headdress; a wizard's cloak and hat (if available); magic wands; tinsel; assorted envelopes containing large and small laminated stars; laminated copy of photocopiable page 52.

## What to do

● Before the children arrive, place large and small stars in envelopes for the children to add together (allowing at least three envelopes per child). Adapt the number of stars you use according to the ability of the children. Put the envelopes into the fantasy box.
● Build up the excitement as you show the children the fantasy box. Encourage them to guess what might be inside and how the

box came to be there. Ask them to remove the contents, talking about the magic wands, stars, envelopes and dressing-up items. Choose one child to wear the fairy skirt or wizard's cloak and to carry a wand.
● Invite the wizard or fairy to tap the box lid with the wand and say, *Abracadabra!* before taking an envelope out of the box, and giving it to one child in the group. The child should count how many big stars and small stars there are inside. Ask the child to tell you how many stars there are altogether. Put into words what they have found. For example: *There is one big star and two small stars. That makes three stars altogether.* Tell the children that if they look at the 'Magic numbers card' they will find the number 3. Work out together that the magic

### Learning objectives
**Calculating**
● Find the total number of items in two groups by counting all of them. **(PSRN)**
**Early Learning Goal**
● Begin to relate addition to combining two groups of objects and subtraction as taking away. **(PSRN)**

number 3 means the child should *Hop, hop, hop*. Repeat the activity with the rest of the group.

● Adapt the activity to use for subtraction. As the children open the envelopes and count the stars, the wizard or fairy should come along, count a number of the stars, touching each one with the wand and take them away. The children count how many are left. Reinforce what has happened by re-telling as a story. For example: *There were five stars. The fairy took three away. There are two left.*

## Support and extension

● Encourage younger children to place the big stars and small stars in rows before counting them and support them in using the 'Magic numbers card'.
● Put ten or more stars in the envelopes for older children, encouraging them to use the vocabulary associated with addition and subtraction.

## Further activities

● Cut out numerals 1 to 9 in gold foil. Laminate and add these to the fantasy box.

Invite the children to choose a numeral, count and place the corresponding number of stars next to it and then put the stars and numeral into a bag ready for the wizard and fairy to use.

● Put a large number of stars on a table and tell older children that the wizard and needs their help. He needs to find the quickest way to count the stars. If they need guidance, suggest that the children group the stars in twos, fives or tens to count them.

## Play link

Provide card, star templates, shiny paper and glitter to encourage children to create their own props to add to the fantasy box. **(CD)**

## Home link

Suggest that parents or carers use everyday items to help their children understand adding and taking away, such as counting different fruits in a bowl and finding the total.

### Cross-curricular links
**Developing Imagination and Imaginative Play**
● Play alongside other children who are engaged in the same theme. **(CD)**
**Early Learning Goal**
● Use their imagination in art and design, music, dance, imaginative and role play and stories. **(CD)**

# Magic numbers card

**1.** Jump, jump jump.

**2.** Run, run, run.

**3.** Hop, hop, hop.

**4.** Clap, clap, clap.

**5.** Stamp, stamp, stamp.

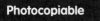

# The toolbox

**When two play vehicles break down in the outside play area, children have lots of opportunities to practise the language of size and position when using the tools they find in the toolbox.**

**Early mathematicians** begin to understand and use the language of size and position, working alongside an adult as they take on the role of car mechanics.
**More confident mathematicians** work independently as they follow instructions involving the language of size and position.

## What you need

A toolbox labelled '123 Garage', containing: pretend tools such as pliers, hammer, spanner, nuts, bolts, wrench, torch and battery-operated drill/ screwdriver; notepad; pen; pretend mobile phone. Also needed: ride-on vehicles; real mobile phone; overalls (if available).

## What to do

● Before the session, place two of the ride-on vehicles (such as cars or motorbikes) on the outdoor play area.
● Show the children the toolbox and ask them who they think would use the equipment inside. Establish that the toolbox must belong to the 123 Garage and be used when a mechanic is repairing a

vehicle. Encourage the children to name and handle the different tools and work out how to use those that are battery-operated. Talk about the size of the tools and ask the children to pick out the longest and shortest, placing them in a row in order of length. Emphasise that these are pretend tools and the children should not touch real tools as they may hurt themselves.
● While you are talking to the children, arrange for another adult to telephone you on a mobile phone. Note down a message that two vehicles have broken down outside and need repairing. Tell the children that someone needs help and this is their chance to be mechanics. Give them overalls to wear and send them out with the toolbox to

### Learning objectives
**Shape, Space and Measures**
● Observe and use positional language. **(PSRN)**
● Are beginning to understand 'bigger than' and 'enough'. **(PSRN)**
**Early Learning Goals**
● Use everyday words to describe position. **(PSRN)**
● Use language such as 'circle' or 'bigger' to describe the shape and size of solids and flat shapes. **(PSRN)**

help repair the ride-on vehicles. Play alongside the children, encouraging use of the language of position and size, using words such as *under, over, above, inside, longer, shorter, bigger* and *smaller.*

### Support and extension
● Model the use of positional and size language when playing alongside younger children.
● Give older children instructions involving the use of positional and size language such as: *Check under the car; Look inside the engine* or *Use the biggest spanner.*

### Further activities
● Share non-fiction books about vehicles with the children and ask them to choose one vehicle that they would like to make. Use a very large cardboard box (such as those used for large electrical appliances) to make a vehicle that is big enough for the children to fit inside. Tape or glue boxes and cardboard wheels to this. Cut doors in the sides and paint it when completed. Encourage the children to use the language of position and size as they make the

vehicle (and afterwards in their play).
● Ask the children to help you think of a way of making a checklist of the tools in the toolbox, so that none are lost. This could be a small book with a drawing of a tool on each page, a set of photographs, a laminated poster with labelled drawings, or photocopies of each tool that are then cut out and stuck onto thick card to create a 'shadow board' that the children can use to match the correct tool to its 'shadow'.

### Play link
Provide small cars, a large cardboard box and paints for the children to make a model of the 123 Garage to use in their play. **(CD)**

### Home link
Suggest that parents or carers take the opportunity to use a trip to the park as a way of helping their children understand words associated with position, such as *under, over, through, on top of* or *underneath.*

> **Cross-curricular links**
> **Using Equipment and Materials**
> ● Use one-handed tools and equipment. **(PD)**
> **Early Learning Goal**
> ● Handle tools, objects, construction and malleable materials safely and with increasing control. **(PD)**

# The sewing box

Children learn about size and shape as they explore a sewing box
and make decorated blankets that are the perfect sizes to keep
Big Bear and Little Bear warm.

## What you need

A box containing: a laminated copy of photocopiable page 57; a small teddy bear; a larger teddy bear; pieces of fabric in assorted sizes; pieces of felt in assorted shapes (squares, circles, triangles, rectangles); large-eyed needles; scissors; assorted threads.

## What to do

● Show the children the box and ask them to speculate about what might be inside. Reveal the contents, encouraging the children to examine each item, talking about and naming the mathematical felt shapes and discussing the sizes of the bears. Remind them of the safety aspects of using needles and scissors. Read the 'Teddy bear card' together.
● Decide together how to make a blanket to keep one of the bears warm. Give the children time to sort and talk about big and small pieces of fabric and the properties of the mathematical felt shapes. Encourage them to choose or cut a piece of fabric that is the appropriate size to make a blanket for one of the bears. Ask: *Is it long enough? Is it wide enough?* Encourage them to embellish the felt shapes by sewing long and short stitches and to sew or glue these to the 'blanket'.

> **Early mathematicians** begin to understand the language of size and talk about shapes.
> **More confident mathematicians** develop their language and understanding as they name mathematical shapes and sew with long and short stitches.

> **Learning objectives**
> **Shape, Space and Measures**
> ● Show curiosity about and observation of shapes by talking about how they are the same or different. **(PSRN)**
> **Early Learning Goal**
> ● Use language such as 'circle' or 'bigger' to describe the shape and size of solids and flat shapes. **(PSRN)**

● Take a photograph of the bear covered in the finished blanket and keep this in the sewing box for reference.

## Support and extension

● Support younger children in understanding the concepts of big and small, long and short.
● Challenge older children to decorate the blanket with 'only shapes with straight sides' or 'all the big circles'.

## Further activity

Provide assorted felt circles and threads on a colour theme such as 'sunshine'. Ask the children to choose and decorate circles using long and short stitches. Mount the circles close together to make one piece of art work.

## Play link

Provide teddy bears and dolls of different sizes, cardboard boxes for beds, scissors and scraps of fabric to enable the children to make blankets of appropriate sizes for the bears and dolls. **(KUW)**

## Home link

Suggest that parents or carers encourage their children to talk about shape and size in everyday situations, such as making sandwiches in different shapes and sizes.

> **Cross-curricular links**
> **Designing and Making**
> ● Use simple tools and techniques competently and appropriately. **(KUW)**
> **Early Learning Goal**
> ● Select the tools and techniques they need to shape, assemble and join materials they are using. **(KUW)**

# Teddy bear card

Hello!
I am **Big Bear**.
I am cold.
Can you make a
**big** blanket to
keep me warm?

Hello!
I am **Little Bear.**
I am cold too!
Can you make a
**small** blanket to
keep me warm?

# The farmer's box

**When the children open the farmer's box they find a letter asking them to help rescue a sheep stranded on an island. They help by creating structures using 2D and 3D shapes.**

**Early mathematicians** begin to use mathematical language and solve problems, with support, using 2D and 3D shapes.
**More confident mathematicians** develop mathematical language and ideas as they work together to solve problems involving 2D and 3D shapes.

## What you need

A box containing: laminated copy of photocopiable page 60; small-world sheep, tractor and trailer; circle of green paper approximately 30cm in diameter (to make an island); length of shiny blue fabric (to make the sea around the island); selection of 2D and 3D shapes; pieces of card, scissors; sticky tape; string. Also needed: digital camera.

## What to do

● When preparing the box, set the scene with a sheep on the island and use the contents of the box to make and photograph simple structures showing ways that the children could rescue the sheep. These may be simple bridges or a boat pulled across the water with string. Put the photos in an envelope inside the box.

● Tell the children that the box has been left by a farmer who needs their help. Will they try to help him?

● Open the box, read the note and talk about the picture. Set the scene by placing the sheep onto the green paper and surrounding it by 'water' as you drape the fabric around the island. Explain to the children that the sheep is on an island surrounded by water and it cannot swim to safety. Ask: *Can you think of ways to rescue the sheep using the*

**Learning objectives**
**Shape, Space and Measures**
● Show interest by sustained construction activity or by talking about shapes or arrangements. **(PSRN)**
● Begin to use mathematical names for 'solid' 3D shapes and 'flat' 2D shapes and mathematical terms to describe shapes. **(PSRN)**
**Early Learning Goals**
● Use language such as 'circle' or 'bigger' to describe the shape and size of solids and flat shapes. **(PSRN)**
● Use developing mathematical ideas and methods to solve practical problems. **(PSRN)**

*things in the box?* Only introduce the photos if the children need more help with ideas.

● Examine the contents of the box together, talking about and naming the 2D and 3D shapes. Encourage the children to experiment and build structures with the shapes, talking about their ideas and commenting on which shapes will stack easily. Encourage the use of language to describe size and position such as *bigger, smaller, on top of, under, over* and *inside.* Help the children tape the shapes and pieces of card together until they have a stable structure to 'walk' the sheep over to safety. They can then put it in the trailer and drive it back to the farm.

● Photograph the end results and add the photos to the farmer's box.

## Support and extension

● Show the photos of structures to younger children and support them in making something similar and talking about the shapes they use.

● Encourage older children to work together trying out their ideas and talking about what they are doing.

## Further activities

● Provide a collection of assorted large toy animals and 3D shapes. Play alongside the children, setting challenges: *Can you build a wall taller than the giraffe? Can you find a shape longer than the snake? Can you find a shape that the monkey can roll?*

● Encourage the children to use talk to pretend imaginary situations by asking: *How did the sheep get onto the island in the first place?*

## Play link

Provide a variety of cardboard boxes, card, scissors, sticky tape and string. Include soft toy farm animals to encourage the children to create bridges, walkways and homes for the animals. **(KUW)**

## Home link

Suggest that parents or carers point out to their children any bridges over water, railways or roads in their local area.

### Cross-curricular links
**Using Equipment and Materials**
● Engage in activities requiring hand-eye coordination. **(PD)**
**Early Learning Goal**
● Handle tools, objects, construction and malleable materials safely and with control. **(PD)**

# The farmer's box

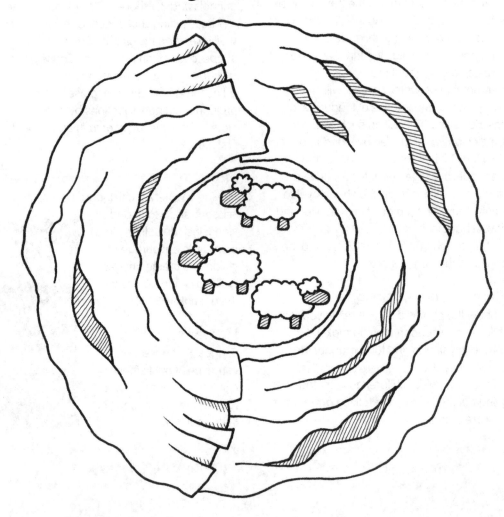

Dear children,

Please can you help me rescue my sheep?

Thank you.

www.scholastic.co.uk

# The cook's box

**Children have fun when they look inside the cook's box and find the ingredients to make cheese shapes. They follow pictorial instructions, weigh the ingredients, make and eat the cheese shapes.**

**Early mathematicians** begin to understand the concept of 'heavy' and 'light' and use mathematical shape cutters.
**More confident mathematicians** follow numbered instructions as they weigh ingredients, name shapes and use a timer.

## What you need

Lidded plastic box containing: self-raising flour; cheddar cheese; butter; one egg; pinch of salt; strips of red, yellow and green pepper; laminated copy of photocopiable page 63; digital camera. Also needed: digital or balance scales; bowls; whisk; rolling pin; circle-, triangle- and square-shaped cutters; baking tray; oven.

## What to do

● Before undertaking the activity, check for any allergies or particular dietary requirements. Make sure that surfaces are safe for food preparation. Keep perishable goods refrigerated until needed.
● Show the children the box and tell them that before they open it they must wash their hands and put on clean aprons. Does this give them a clue about what they will be doing? Open the box and ask the children to identify and talk about the contents. Encourage them to smell and taste a little of the cheese and peppers. Ask them if they can think of anything they could make using all of the ingredients.
● Read and talk about the step-by-step instructions on the photocopiable sheet. Ask the children to refer to the pictures and select the equipment they will need. Tell them that you will take photographs as they are working. Ask them to handle the wrapped ingredients. Ask: *Which is the heaviest? Is the bag of flour lighter than the piece of cheese?* Help the children weigh the following ingredients using digital or balance scales:

**Learning objectives**
**Shape, Space and Measures**
● Order two items by weight or capacity.
**(PSRN)**
**Early Learning Goal**
● Use language such as 'greater', 'smaller', 'heavier' or 'lighter' to compare quantities.
**(PSRN)**

200g self-raising flour
150g cheddar cheese
100g butter

● Use language such as *a bit more, too much* and *about right*. Follow the numbered steps on the instruction card until Step 5. Show the children the different-shaped cutters and encourage them to name the circle, triangle and square. Help them to make a selection of cheese shapes and decorate them with strips of pepper. Set a timer for ten minutes and bake the shapes at 180°C or Gas Mark 4. Challenge the children to complete the washing-up in ten minutes, before the timer rings. When the cheese shapes are cooked and have cooled, ask the children to tell you how they have changed during cooking. Enjoy the cheese shapes at snack time.

## Support and extension

● Give younger children extra time to handle the ingredients to understand the concepts of heavy and light.
● Challenge older children to follow the pictorial instructions more independently, using mathematical language to explain what they are doing, and why.

## Further activities

● Print the photographs of the activity. Ask the children to help you place them in the correct order, using language such as *before, after, next*. Stick the photographs onto a strip of card and number them together. Keep them in the cook's box.
● Share a selection of simple children's cookery books and ask the children to find a picture of something else they would like to make. Include the ingredients and recipe in the cook's box as a surprise for the children next time they have the opportunity to cook.

## Play link

Provide scales, a timer, play dough, shape cutters, rolling pins and coloured matchsticks to use as decoration, for children to make pretend cheese shapes in the role-play kitchen. **(CD)**

## Home link

Suggest that parents or carers include their children in weighing and baking activities at home.

### Cross-curricular links
**Exploration and Investigation**
● Show an awareness of change. **(KUW)**
**Early Learning Goal**
● Look closely at similarities, differences, patterns and change. **(KUW)**

Open the box!

# Make cheese shapes

1. Weigh

2. Rub

3. Mix

4. Roll

5. Cut

6. Decorate and bake

Maths without worksheets

**SCHOLASTIC**
www.scholastic.co.uk

## In this series:

**Writing without pencils**
Writing with torches, icing, fingers and more
Brenda Whittle
For ages 3-5
ISBN 978-0439-94499-1

**Painting without brushes**
Painting with leaves, hands, wellies and more.
Brenda Whittle
For ages 3-5
ISBN 978-0439-94515-8

**Reading without realising**
Reading signs, lists, letters and more
Brenda Whittle and Heidi Jayne
For ages 3-5
ISBN 978-0439-94556-1

**ICT without a PC**
ICT with cameras, floor robots and more
Brenda Whittle and Heidi Jayne
For ages 3-5
ISBN 978-0439-94555-4

**Maths without worksheets**
Maths through painting, role play and more
Brenda Whittle and Heidi Jayne
For ages 3-5
ISBN 978-0439-94558-5

**Speaking without hesitation**
Rhymes, discussions, role play and more
Brenda Whittle and Heidi Jayne
For ages 3-5
ISBN 978-0439-94557-8

To find out more, call: 0845 603 9091
or visit our website www.scholastic.co.uk